Journey With Joy
I0695499

Harness Heights

Heart
Hustle
Honor

Stay
Strive
Shine!

ENGAGE
EVERY
ESSENCE

DRIVE
DEFINES
DESTINY

Steadfast
In
Spirit

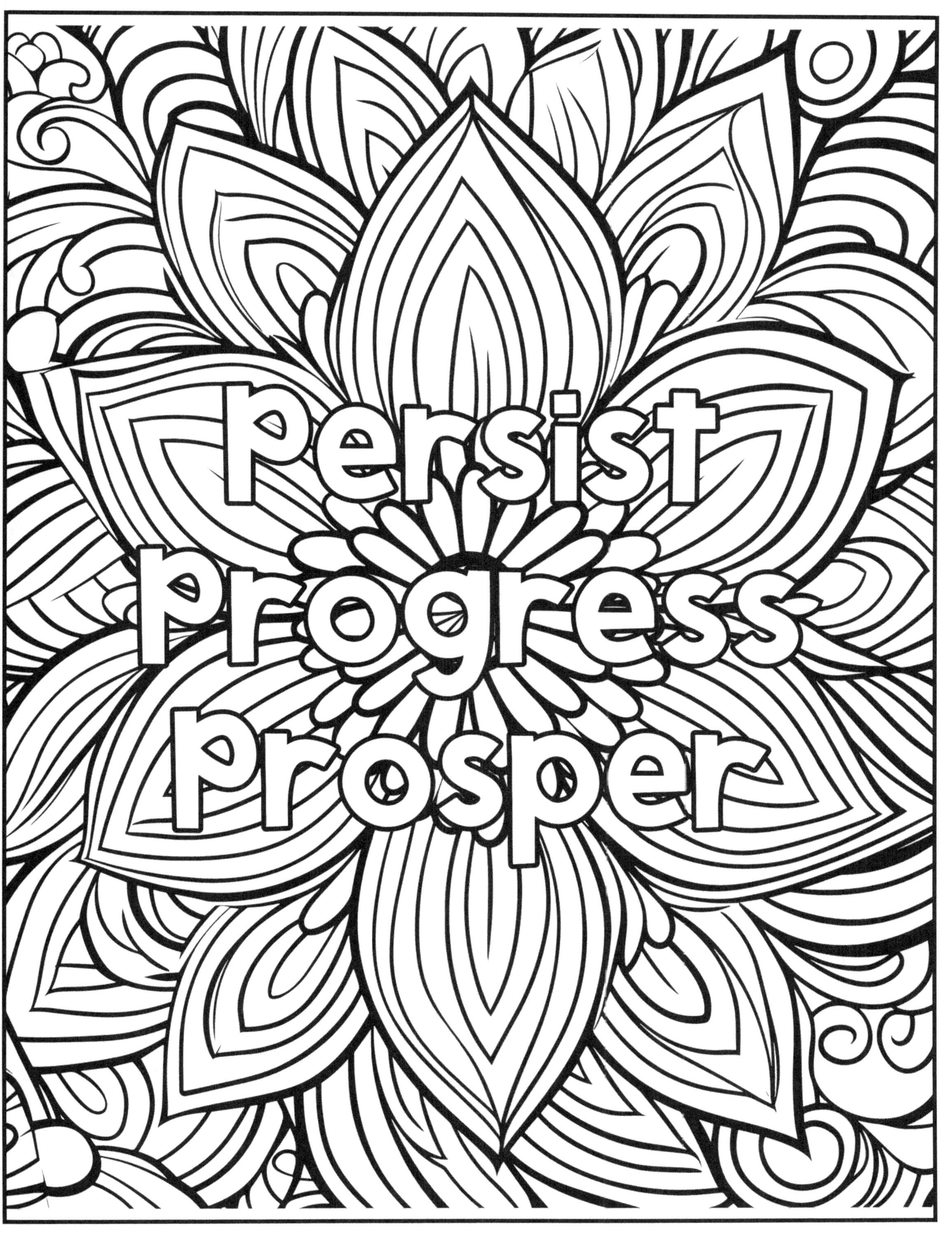

persist
progress
prosper

Liberate
Lofty
Limits

REACH
FOR
THE
STARS

Awaken
Ambitions
Ardently

Driven
By
Dreams

Bravely
Breach
Barriers

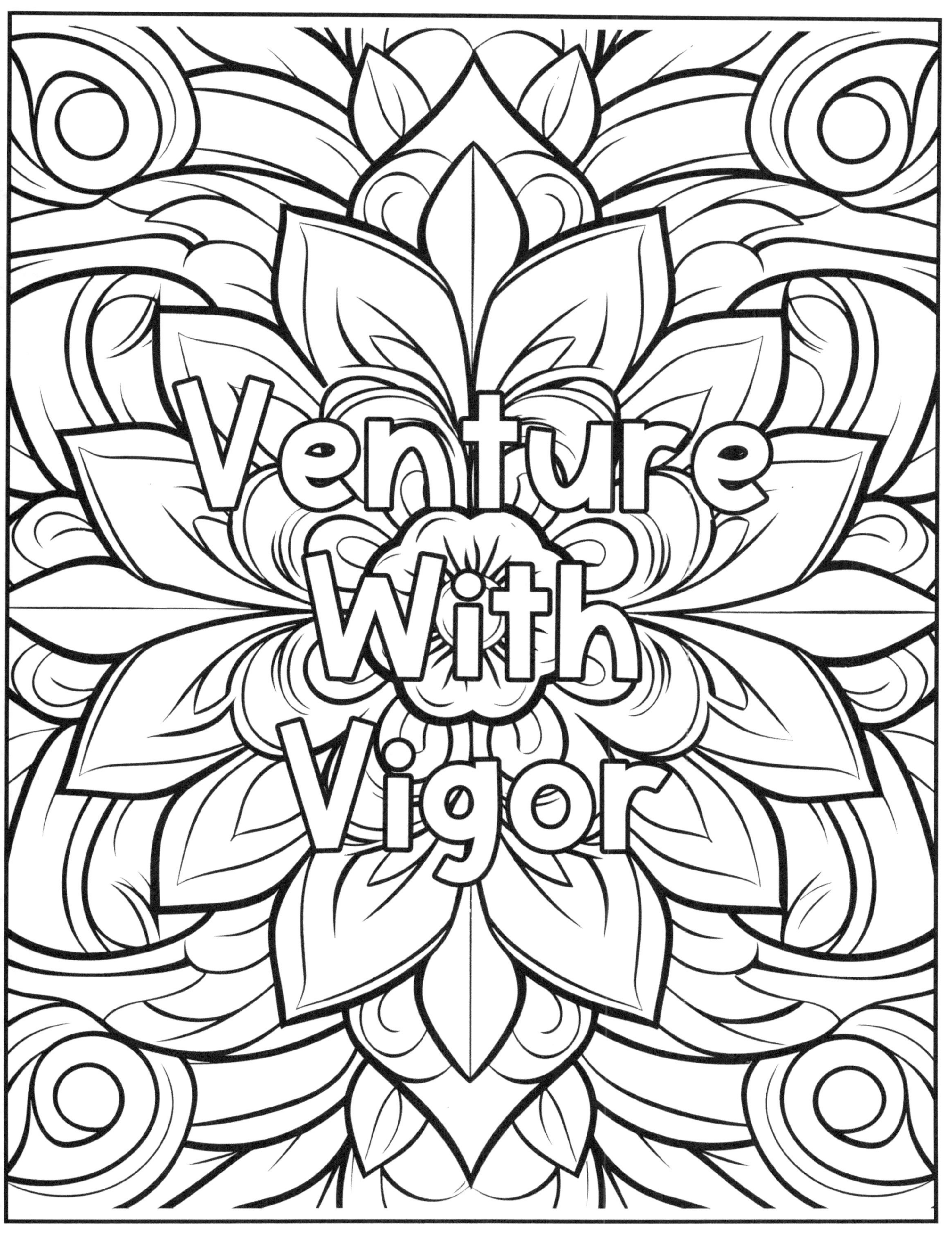

Venture
With
Vigor

Tango
With
Tenacity

Nestle
In
Newfound
Notions

Hold
The
Horizon

Steadfast
Stay
Strong

Unearth
Untold
Universes

HONOR
HEARTFELT
HUNGERS

Legacy
Of
Self-love

Celebrate
Your
Core

Master
Your
Mindset

INWARD
INSIGHT
OUTWARD
IMPACT

Stitch
Strength
To
Soul

Trust Your Instincts

IGNITE
INSPIRE
IMPACT

Believe
To
Achieve

Venture
With
Valor

Kickstart
Kinetic
Kicks

Empower
Your
Journey

YOU'RE
YOUR
OWN
COMPASS

Gather
Grow
Glow

Move
With
Meaning

Vocalize
Vibrant
Victories

Wield
Winsome
Wisdom

WIELD
YOUR
WONDER

Find
Fortitude

Harbor
Heartfelt
Hopes

Never
Negate
Your
Nature

FOSTER
FORWARD
FOCUS

Empower Every Echo

Valor In Every Venture

Luminous
Legacy
Lives